Freedom Day: A Juneteenth Celebration
Copyright © 2024 by Brown Butterfly Press, LLC
All rights reserved. No part of this publication may be reproduced, distributed, or transmitted in any form or by any means, including photographing, recordings, or electronic or mechanical methods without the written permission of the publisher, except with critical reviews and noncommercial uses permitted by copyright law.

SScan the QR code to explore more Brown Butterfly Books, join Renée's email list, or purchase signed copies.

ISBN: 978-1-960528-15-5 Paperback
ISBN: 978-1-960528-16-2 Hardcover
Library of Congress Control Number: 2024909683

dedicated to all the children and adults, both those who celebrate freedom and those who have not yet discovered its significance. May this book help you learn the importance of Juneteenth and ways to celebrate the unity and strength in diversity. Let us honor the ancestors whose resilience and courage paved the way to the freedom of African Americans in America.

This book belongs to

_____
_____

Freedom Day
A Juneteenth Celebration

Renée Ecckles-Hardy

Welcome to Juneteenth! It is a special day when we celebrate freedom.

Long ago, many people were not free.
But then, something important happened.

On June 19, 1865, enslaved people in Texas learned they were free. That is why we celebrate Juneteenth!

Families come together on Juneteenth. We share delicious food like barbecue, cornbread, and watermelon.

We make Juneteenth flags with red, black, and green. There is also a traditional flag with red, white, and blue. Each color has a special meaning.

Communities have parades and festivals. We celebrate with music, dancing, and games.

Juneteenth reminds us of our past, celebrates our freedom, and brings us together as one big family.

Families share stories about our ancestors. We learn about their bravery and strength.

We honor our ancestors by planting seeds of hope for the future.

We express our creativity by making art that celebrates freedom and unity.

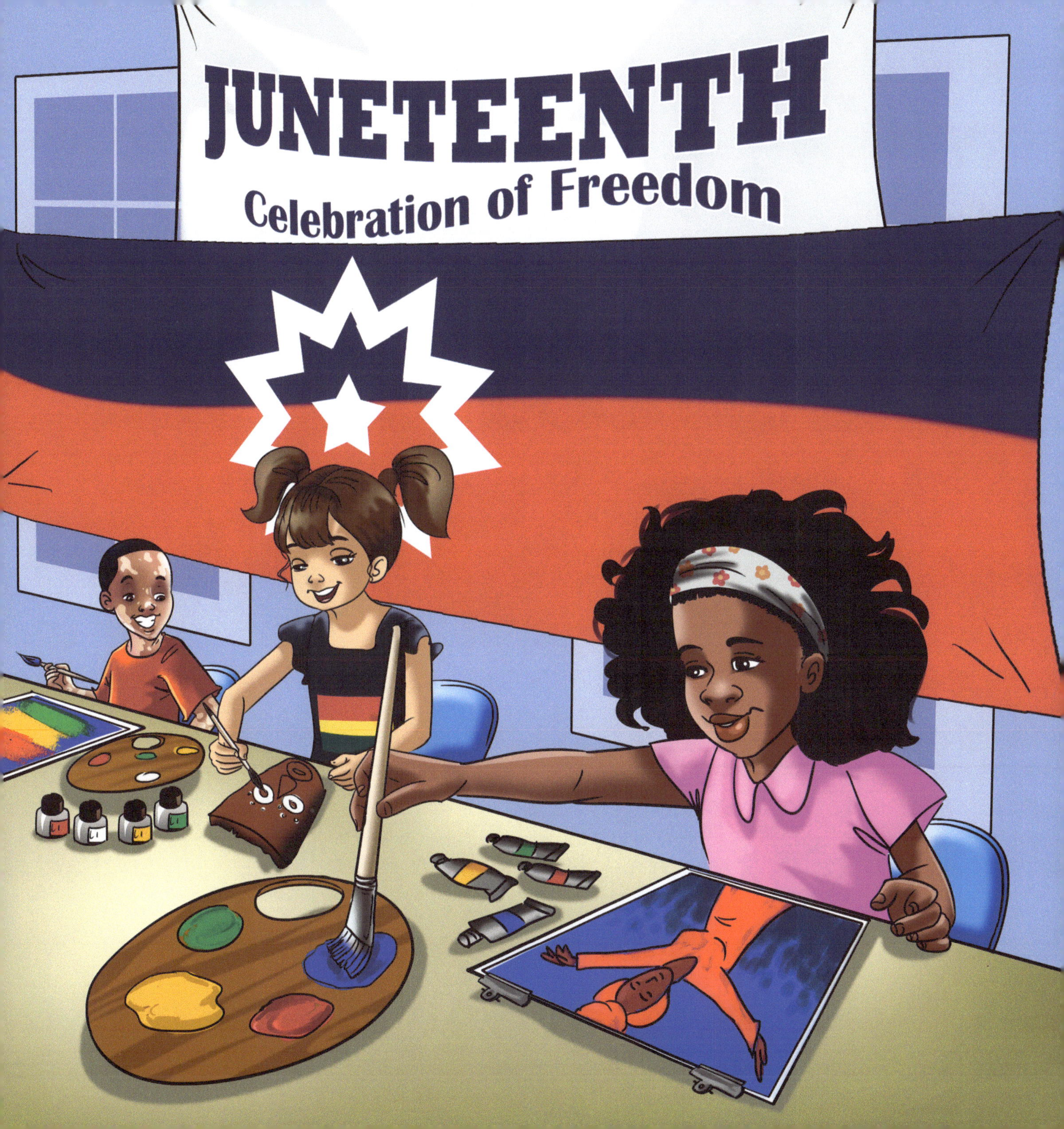
JUNETEENTH
Celebration of Freedom

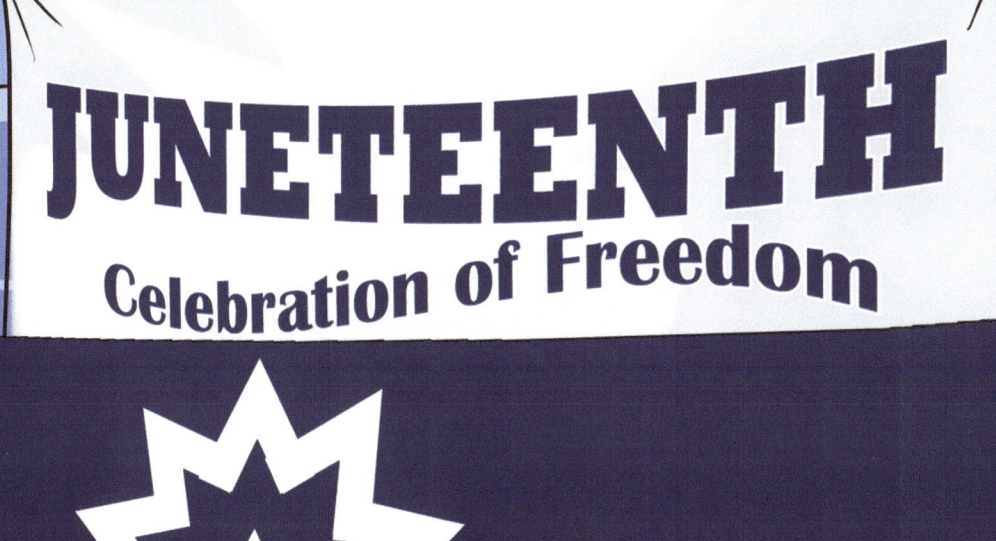

We learn about Juneteenth and African American history through books and stories.

We stand united against injustice and oppression, working together for equality and justice.

Thank you for learning about Juneteenth with us! Let us keep celebrating and spreading joy together.

What does freedom mean to you? Take a moment to think about it.

Glossary of Terms:

Juneteenth: A holiday celebrated on June 19th each year, commemorating the emancipation of enslaved African Americans in the United States.

Emancipation Proclamation: A presidential proclamation issued by President Abraham Lincoln on January 1, 1863, declaring that all enslaved persons in Confederate-held territory were to be set free.

Freedom: The power or right to act, speak, or think as one wants without hindrance or restraint, often associated with the absence of slavery, oppression, or coercion.

Unity: The state of being united or joined together as one, often in purpose or action, as demonstrated by the children holding hands in the story.

Celebration: A joyful and festive gathering or event, often held in honor of a special occasion or milestone, such as Juneteenth.

Community: A group of people living in the same place or having a particular characteristic in common, often with shared interests, values, and goals, as depicted by the families and friends coming together to celebrate Juneteenth.

Ancestors: People from whom one is descended, typically considered as those who lived several generations ago, whose bravery and strength are honored and remembered on Juneteenth.

Bravery: Courageous behavior or actions, especially in the face of danger, difficulty, or adversity, exemplified by the stories of the ancestors shared on Juneteenth.

Resilience: The ability to recover from difficult circumstances and bounce back from challenges, as shown by the planting of seeds of hope for the future.

Justice: The quality of being fair and reasonable, often involving the administration of law or the assignment of punishment or reward according to what is morally right, emphasized by the children standing united against injustice and oppression.

Juneteenth Flags

The Juneteenth flag has special colors and symbols that mean important things.

The star in the middle stands for Texas. This is because people in Galveston, Texas finally learned they were free from slavery on Juneteenth, even though it had ended already.

The star also means freedom for all Black people in America. The bursting shapes around the star show the exciting new freedom Black people had. It looks like when a new bright star is born in the sky.

The curved line across the middle is a symbol of hope and new opportunities for African Americans.

You might also see a red, black, and green flag at Juneteenth celebrations. This is called the Pan-African flag. A group called the Universal Negro Improvement Association picked these colors in 1920 to represent African people.

The red stands for the blood of Africans. The black is for the soil of Africa. The green means prosperity and wealth for the African people.

Recommended Readings for Children Ages 6-10:

1. "All Different Now: Juneteenth, the First Day of Freedom" by Angela Johnson
    - This beautifully illustrated picture book tells the story of Juneteenth from the perspective of a young girl experiencing freedom for the first time.

2. "Juneteenth for Mazie" by Floyd Cooper
    - Through captivating illustrations, this book follows Mazie as she learns about Juneteenth and its significance from her family and community.

3. "Juneteenth Jamboree" by Carole Boston Weatherford
    - Join in the celebration with the characters in this rhythmic story, filled with music, food, and joy as they commemorate Juneteenth together.

4. "Freedom's Gifts: A Juneteenth Story" by Valerie Wesley
    - Through the eyes of a young girl named Addy, readers learn about the history and traditions of Juneteenth, celebrating freedom and family.

5. "Lift Every Voice and Sing" by James Weldon Johnson (Illustrated by Elizabeth Catlett)
    - This classic poem, also known as the Black National Anthem, celebrates resilience, unity, and hope, making it a perfect read for Juneteenth.

6. "Juneteenth: A Celebration of Freedom" by Charles Taylor
    - This informative book provides an overview of Juneteenth's history and significance, accompanied by photographs and illustrations.

7. "Juneteenth: Freedom Day" by Muriel Miller Branch
   - Through engaging text and historical photographs, this book explores the events leading up to Juneteenth and its enduring importance.

8. "Moses: When Harriet Tubman Led Her People to Freedom" by Carole Boston Weatherford (Illustrated by Kadir Nelson)
   - Although not specifically about Juneteenth, this book recounts the remarkable story of Harriet Tubman and her efforts to lead enslaved people to freedom, highlighting themes of bravery and liberation.

9. "The Story of Juneteenth: An Interactive History Adventure" by Steven Otfinoski
   - This interactive book allows readers to choose their own path through the history of Juneteenth, engaging them in the learning process.

10. "Freedom's Wings: Corey's Diary" by Sharon Dennis Wyeth
    - Through the diary entries of a young boy named Corey, readers learn about the challenges and triumphs of African Americans during the Civil War and beyond, including the significance of Juneteenth.

**(Note: This condensed version of the story maintains the key elements of Juneteenth